The Buttercup Game

Lee Sterrey

Written by

Lee Sterrey

Illustrated by

Nicola Wyldbore-Smith

First published: January 2016

ISBN-10: 1523343052

ISBN-13: 978-1523343058

This Adventure on Honey Bee Farm is dedicated to

the carers.

Grady Grey loved to visit his Nana, she was so much fun.
Nana played with him and would chase him in the sun.

They'd bounce in circles and had lots of time to play.
"Look at how high I can jump!" shouted Grady Grey.

He'd jump over the buttercups, leaping high into the air.
"Well Done!" Nana cheered,
"You just jumped higher than a Hare!"

Once they were home,
Grady Grey would ask his mum,
"When can we visit Nana again?
She is so much fun."

At last! It was time to visit Nana,
Grady Grey said, "Come on, let's go!"
But instead his mummy said,
"There is something you need to know.

Remember when Nana forgot
where she had put the lettuce for us to eat?"
Grady Grey laughed, "Yes, it took ages to find,
but we found it under a seat."

"Recently," Mummy continued, "Nana's forgot quite alot.
She forgets where she lives and what she has got.

Yesterday, cousin Beatrice, found Nana near the Fox den.
Luckily, Beatrice stopped her and took her home again.

Nana is quite poorly and she needs some special care.
I wanted to tell you this, before I take you there."

"Oh no! Yesterday I forgot to put my dirty clothes away!
Am I getting poorly too?" Asked a worried Grady Grey.

Mummy smiled, "No Grady Grey, that's not the same.
Nana has an illness and it is that which is to blame."

"What about special medicine, that's made from a nettle?"
Asked Grady Grey, "All we need to do is boil it in a kettle."

Mummy replied, "My medicine won't help this time.
Let me explain, what's happening in Nana's mind."

Mummy drew a circle upon the warren floor and said,
"Think of this as looking inside Nana's head."

Mummy drew a smaller circle, then picked up a stone,
"Now imagine this pebble is a Thought buzzing all alone.

Inside this smaller circle is Nana's memory,
where she remembers things, including you and me."

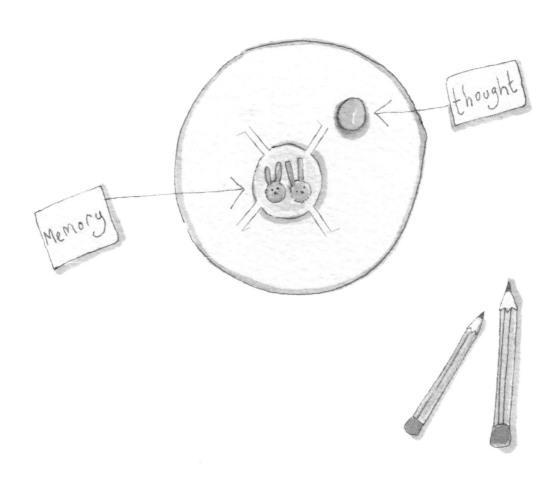

Grady Grey asked, "Is tickle my tummy memory in there?"
"Yes." replied Mummy, "And you dressed as a bear…

Now see the lines from 'memory' that are set out straight?
Notice that each one of them has a little gate?

These lines help the Thought get into the memory.
But sometimes the gates close
and Thoughts get lost, you see?"

"Now get those lovely cupcakes, made by Jessica Mouse.

It is time to set off and visit Nana at her house."

Nana opened her door and gave Grady Grey a big smile.
"Hello!" She said "Come on in! It's been such a long while!

We can have a… oh what's that word? I'm such a clown.
I just can't remember." Nana's smile turned into a frown.

Grady Grey was worried and whispered to his Mummy,
"Nana's Thought got lost. She can't remember Grassy-Tea."

Grady Grey said, "I can get some grass to be churned."
"Grassy-Tea are the words!" And Nana's smile returned.

They all had tea and cakes, which were very yummy.
"What's the news on Honey Bee Farm?" asked Mummy.

"Did you hear about Betsy the Bantam?" Nana replied.
"Betsy fooled the Fox!" She said with enormous pride.

"I heard that Betsy was very clever."
Mummy joyfully said,
 "Did you hear that the pigs
had escaped from their bed?"

Nana chuckled. "Not again!
I bet they dug under the gate!
It's always how those naughty pigs,
manage to escape!"

"Did you hear about Betsy the Bantam?"
Nana asked again.
"She fooled the Fox with a Fine Nose
and stayed out of his den."

Nana asked the same question and it confused Grady Grey.
"Mummy, Nana's lost her Thought, what should we say?"

"We answer it again." His mummy whispered fast.
"Nana doesn't know it's something she has already asked."

Nana asked it over again and Grady Grey soon got bored.
He fidgeted and got annoyed, with the Nana he adored.

Mummy noticed and said, "Lets go outside to play.
How high can we jump over the buttercups today?"

"What a lovely idea." replied Nana.
"Let me get my shawl,
I will only be a minute,
it is hanging in the hall."

After some time Mummy said,
"Nana's been quite long."
"She's in the hall!" Grady Grey replied,
"But something's very wrong."

Nana was stood in the corner and hid like a tiny mouse. "Who are you?" She asked. "Please leave my house."

"Oh no," Grady Grey whispered,
"Nana's forgotten us too.
Her Thought's got lost again,
on it's way to remember me and you."

Mummy quietly said,
"This is your grandson, Grady Grey.
We've come to visit you
and jump over buttercups today."

Nana wasn't sure,
but agreed to watch the bunny jump high.
Grady Grey boasted,
"I'm so good I can touch the sky!"

He bounded in circles
and spent loads of time in play.
"Look at how high I can jump!"
shouted Grady Grey.

He jumped over the buttercups
leaping high into the air.
Nana's smile returned and she cheered,
"You just jumped higher… than a Hare!"

When the sun started
to get very low in the sky,
It was time for Grady Grey
and his Nana to say goodbye.

On the way home,
Grady Grey said to his mum,
"I know things are different now,
but we still had lots of fun.

I'm sad that Nana
won't always remember my name,
but I'm glad that she enjoyed me playing
The Buttercup Game."

Mummy smiled "Nana will sometimes forget we're there.
But something she'll always love to see again,
is you jump higher than a Hare."

More Adventures on
Honey Bee Farm

Doyley the Dormouse

Written by Lee Sterrey Illustrated by Nicola Wyldbore-Smith

The Escaped Pig

Written by Lee Sterrey Illustrated by Nicola Wyldbore-Smith

Doyley the Dormouse
is the best door-maker in town,
but how does he make one that isn't round?

www.facebook.com/DoyleytheDormouse

The Pig has escaped again!
Just how will Piccolo the Hound and Pogo the Filly
get him back to his pen?

www.facebook.com/TheEscapedPig

A note from the Author, Lee Sterrey:

"I was inspired to write 'The Buttercup Game' when a friend once demanded of me through her tears, that if I could do something to help families and carers of people with Dementia, then I must.

I hope this helps."

www.AdventuresOnHoneyBeeFarm.com

About the Illustrator, Nicola Wyldbore-Smith

Nicola gains much of her inspiration for her illustrations from the beautiful Warwickshire (UK) countryside in which she resides. Having kept many animals including horses, sheep and dogs she captures the natural movement and expressions of animals in her illustrations.

For Adventures on Honey Bee Farm stories, Nicola creates her drawings first in pencil and then uses watercolour paints to get that lovely delicate finish that can only be obtained by hand painting.

Each finished artwork is a masterpiece in it's own right.

Made in the USA
Charleston, SC
27 February 2016